The Secrets of "Sell-A-Million Sam"

SAMUEL E. GROSS

Copyright © 2014

All rights reserved.

ISBN: 1505511070
ISBN-13: 978-1505511079

CONTENTS

Foreword 2

Introduction 5

Chapter 1. My wisest investment in human relations 7

Chapter 2. Short cuts to better buying 9

Chapter 3. The new buyer takes over . . . now what? 15

Chapter 4. Putting the "show" in showmanship 20

Chapter 5. Private brand for extra profits 23

Chapter 6. Speeding up slow-moving merchandise 25

Chapter 7. Promotions spell p-r-o-f-i-t 27

Chapter 8. How to buy and then sell close-outs 30

Chapter 9. Chalking up record sales with a recorder 34

Chapter 10. This little buyer went to market 37

Chapter 11. My miracle sales chart 40

Chapter 12. Mistakes you can easily avoid 42

Chapter 13. My little black book 45

Chapter 14. Getting your salesclerks to sell 48

Chapter 15. What about the customer 51

Chapter 16. When you think you've arrived, you've ceased to climb 56

Chapter 17. If I were a small retailer 59

Chapter 18. He started as a stock boy 62

Chapter 19. What's ahead and how to face it 63

Chapter 20. One hundred steps to sales success 69

Foreword

On the day I first met Sam Gross I was struck by one commanding quality: his unbridled enthusiasm. This is not an uncommon trait among people in retailing, but in Sam's case it was so outstanding as to be noteworthy. He was obviously an eager young man, anxious to get ahead. It was equally apparent that he was capable, having started out as a stock boy when only a teenager in Chicago and later assuming a buyer's responsibilities with a reputable Chicago firm. But aside from all that, the thing that most stood out about Sam Gross was his enthusiasm.

That was 38 years ago. Since that time I have never ceased to be amazed at the fervor with which he attacks every undertaking that comes his way.

During his almost four decades of loyal service with Famous-Barr Company, Sam has carved an enviable reputation for himself. No doubt his own innate ability, coupled with hard work and enthusiasm, were largely responsible for the formation of his successful career. But along with these, there was Sam's capacity for inspiring those who worked with him. He was a maker of top salesmen, junior executives and merchandise men. Generously and freely he shared with these people the many secrets of his success, secrets that won for him the appellation of "Sell-A-Million Sam."

Those same secrets are revealed in the pages that follow. They should be of immense value to anyone connected with the great profession known as retailing, particularly those newcomers who, up until the publication of this book, have not had the good fortune of knowing Sam Gross.

Morton J. May
Chairman, Board of Directors
The May Department Stores Company
St. Louis June, 1961

To his three adoring grandchildren he's known as "Grandpa," to his business acquaintances in the Orient he's known as "Sam-Sam," to the 150 salespeople who worked for him at Famous-Barr he's known as "Mr. Gross," but to practically everybody else in retailing he's known as "Sell-A-Million Sam." After reading this book, I don't think you'll have any difficulty in understanding how and why Sam Gross earned this latter nickname.

For when Sam retired from Famous-Barr earlier this year after almost forty years, he left behind a record seldom if ever matched in the annals of department store retailing. He was buyer for sporting goods, auto accessories, radio, television, records, cameras and pet supplies for Famous-Barr's downtown store and three branches, as well as chairman of the radio, television and camera buying committees for the entire May Department Stores chain. His achievements in each of these capacities are legendary, and I consider him the greatest showman and best salesman I have known in retailing.

Typical of the buying coups scored by "Sell-A-Million Sam" was the 1950 deal that resulted in Famous-Barr's acquisition of the stock of a bankrupt sporting goods firm in St. Louis. Some of us felt that the stock was too large to be handled profitably by Famous-Barr and the rest of the stores in our Company combined, but Sam persuaded us that he alone could handle almost the entire stock. As a result, thousands flocked to the Famous-Barr sale and, within two weeks, the stock was completely sold out.

This was no easy accomplishment. It required showmanship as well as salesmanship. It required enthusiasm and, above all, hard work.

It's reassuring to know that, in spite of his retirement, Sam is still as active as ever. Testimony to that fact is the book you're about to read, another milestone in the career of an outstandingly successful merchant.

Morton D. May President
The May Department Stores Company
St. Louis June, 1961

Introduction

When I walked confidently into the big downtown store of Famous-Barr Company in St. Louis on that Spring day of March 23. 1923, I not only carried with me quite a reputation as a sizzling salesman and buyer, out of Chicago, but had added a few embellishments of my own.

Now, mind you, I hadn't lied to anyone to get this new and important job as a radio and sporting goods buyer at Famous-Barr; I merely had the courage of my convictions. If there is any lesson I learned in my 50 years of fast-tempo merchandising it was to tell the truth. That's why they pinned the label of "Honest Sam" on me—and it stuck.

I had developed an extremely good record of radio and phonograph sales at Rothschild's in Chicago when I was literally tapped for service at Famous-Barr. It was March of 1923 and I was in the midst of another of my great crystal set promotions. The sets retailed at S3.95 and I was moving them 500 at a time.

At the height of the sale I felt a tap on my shoulder. I turned around, ready to sell some fellow a $5.95 set, only to have him ask me: "'How'd you like to come down to St. Louis and work for Famous-Barr Company?"

Honestly, I didn't care about any new job at the time. I was engrossed in crystal sets and I told this man just that. Did he want a crystal set? If not, please see me some other day. And I went back to selling.

However, I kept the offer in mind and when the smoke of that sale cleared, I checked into the Famous-Barr deal and went down to St. Louis for an interview. They quizzed me about radio merchandising and. after they seemed satisfied, asked: "What other departments do you head besides radio?"

Without hesitation I blurted out: "Sporting goods."

Now this is what I mean by not kidding anyone. Actually I did head sporting goods at Rothschild's, but I had been given that job only the day before I left for St. Louis. The sporting goods buyer had quit and they had said: "Sam, you take over." And I did.

When the May executives heard that I was also a sporting goods buyer, they replied: "Fine, glad to hear that. You can have sporting goods here, too."

All of this was spinning through my mind as I headed for the offices of Col. David May, the founder of Famous-Barr and the man who started the successful May Company chain of outstanding department stores.

Col. May gave me the once-over as I stood before him and finally remarked: "Glad to have you with us—and now that you are here I want you to build me the biggest and best super-heterodyne radio set in St. Louis. I've always wanted one and you're just the man who can do it."

I looked directly at Col. May. His request startled me, but I tried not to show my momentary worry. You see, I knew nothing about radios, I only sold them. So, being the brash young guy that I was, and having that sense of truthfulness about me, I unhesitatingly replied: "Just a minute, Col. May. Did you hire a mechanic or a buyer? I don't know anything about the mechanics of radios; all I know is how to buy and sell them."

Col. May was shocked at the retort, but he smiled and shot back; "You've got something there, young man. I didn't hire a mechanic; I hired a buyer. However, you better be the best buyer I ever had or you're not going to be around long. Lots of luck to you."

Well, I stayed on at Famous-Barr for thirty-eight years before retiring on January 31, 1961. In that time I sold well over a hundred million dollars worth of merchandise. They tabbed me "Sell a Million Sam," and that has been my second most cherished title, for nothing could replace "Honest Sam" in my affection. In my final years I was hitting the seven million mark annually.

When you buy and then clear your counters of that much merchandise in one year's time, you're bound to have enjoyed many exciting and wonderful experiences—experiences that can help others do the same. The lessons I learned, the mistakes I made, the special deals I was able to engineer—all these I share with you.

I've learned that knowledge is most important to business, but sharing knowledge is even more rewarding.

Chapter 1. My wisest investment in human relations

I'm going to get right to the point early and not wander down the aisles. I never had time to waste in my many years of buying and selling; time is too precious, so why hold back any secrets until the end?

I'll tell you right now that nothing will determine your success more than the ability to make friends. Much of this will come naturally since some people are just born to make friends. Others have to work hard at it.

But I want to impress upon people in buying and selling, whether it comes easy or hard: learn to make friends. Plenty of friends. Don't just shine up to the boss. Get everyone to like you, in and out of the store.

You know what did more to make me a talked about, successful merchandiser at big Famous-Barr?

My Christmas breakfasts.

In my first year with the store, I learned that a number of departments held get-togethers at Christmas time. So the first year I invited a few of my employees to my house. Later, we had a small Christmas breakfast at the store.

The idea began to grow

There were only ten or twelve of us the first few years, but then I began thinking: "This is a nice thing. Why limit it to my own people? Why not let in a few other friends. Those who have done me favors, and who might do more in the future?"

So I began inviting people outside my department—a carpenter who put up a shelf or counter for me, an electrician, a credit man (very important people, not the boss—the guy in the department who does all the work) or someone from shipping. I even began inviting the maids, the porters, the elevator girls, the switchboard operators (don't overlook those gals). Anyone who helped us and might be a bigger help later.

The Christmas breakfast began to grow. So I started putting on a show and hired my own talent. For a while we gave away gifts. In addition to my employees, I also invited my major resources. After a while we had to discontinue inviting the suppliers since the breakfasts were getting too big and other departments became a little jealous. I dressed up, gagged it up, had a lot of fun. Everyone got into the spirit of the thing and I had as many as 260 at these affairs, including top brass. I took pictures—and still have them. A wonderful record of these pleasant events.

My breakfasts were the talk of the store. Nothing else made me as well known to more people. But I wasn't looking for personal publicity. Sure, I'm like the next guy; all this made me feel good, but what I was more pleased to receive were the greetings of the "little people" in the store. I found I was getting more service from them than anyone else. My long-distance calls were always placed quickly; my repair jobs were always fixed first; my credit problems were handled promptly and so on down the line.

Remember one thing

Now the important thing is to pay for these things yourself. Don't expect the company to share the cost. This is your own responsibility; either you like people or you don't. If you don't, quit now before it's too late. If you do. share your enthusiasm with them. They like little attentions, too.

The breakfast in December of 1960 was my thirty-seventh. Down the years we had some wonderful times.

Chapter 2. Short cuts to better buying

Probably anybody can be appointed a buyer, but a good buyer spells the difference between profit and loss. I'm speaking primarily of plain and simple buying, not any management responsibilities added to the job. It takes plenty of planning and complete concentration to be of value to your company as a buyer.

Many buyers come from the ranks of successful salesmen. They know their stock and think they know what their customers want. Yet, when confronted with the responsibility of buying, they're astounded that they don't know exactly what, how, when, or how much to buy. They find they can't detect a hot deal when it's offered and can't make up their minds whether or not to trust a distributor or a representative who calls.

It is to these lost souls that I will direct my remarks, based on my many years of learning the hard way—by making mistakes and then recovering.

Be friendly with everyone

First of all, establish pleasant relationships with the companies from whom you buy and with their salesmen. Become an important account. If you are not fortunate to be with a big company that purchases in large quantities, try and turn enough of the business you have over to one salesman so that you make his trip worthwhile. Don't slice your purchases too thin among a lot of salesmen.

When I started—and even years later—I was honest about my experience and placed my problem right in the lap of the fellow who called on me. If the manufacturer was reputable, I was convinced his representative must be the same, and usually he was.

I would admit my unfamiliarity with his line and would ask him to help me buy the right amount at the right price.

"If you were I, how much would you buy and how much would you pay?" I often asked a representative. I'd do this even in my later years. It places the salesman on the spot. In almost every instance, the salesman will come up with the right answer for he knows that to obtain a reorder, he must be careful not to overload me at the outset and must make it possible for my firm to show a reasonable profit.

If a bad deal resulted, I would be more careful with this salesman the next time, but I would not reject any part of the bargain we had made. I have never gone back on my word.

A buyer's word must be his bond.

Sometimes it's necessary for the man to bite the dog, that is, the buyer taking the salesman to lunch. I often did this with salesmen who called on me for the first time. It gave us a chance to get away from the office, relax and become better acquainted. By the time we had finished luncheon I had sized up the salesman and knew I could come to a better understanding. He got to know me, too, and we were able to agree on better terms, maybe an extra inducement or two. If he was the right type, I'd invite him to come to our store the day we placed his product on sale and help us put it over.

Don't forget quality

A second point of importance to good buying is a strong conviction that quality is more important than price. Of course, in our highly competitive market of today, a good buyer must be able to obtain the best quality at the best price. However, I maintain that the best buyers first ask about a product's performance and then about the price. Best prices depend on volume and on close relationships with the producer.

Those buyers who buy price first often find themselves facing counters full of merchandise at the end of the sales season. The lowest price doesn't always mean the quickest and most successful sale.

You must build confidence between buyer and seller so that a factory will come to you with these valued words: "Sam, I've got something special and am stopping here first. No one else has it yet. I've come to you because I respect your ability to spot a good deal and then run with it."

Sometimes, I would be reluctant to buy, believing better conditions should be forthcoming. Fortunately, further concessions were made more often than not after the representative consulted with his home office. Sometimes, though, they'd pass me up and the store down the street would clean up on the item I had snubbed.

But you can't win them all, although you had better not let too many slip away.

A buyer purchases from two major sources:

(1)   From a jobber or distributor.

(2) Direct from the manufacturer.

Of course, there is the private brand, but that is a direct factory deal, too.

Advantages of a jobber

Buying from a jobber has its advantages. You work on his stock and sometimes all you need are a few samples and you can fill in quickly whenever you run low. Jobbers are good protection. In smaller firms, jobbers are often your best bet. They save you money in the long run.

Because of the company I represented, I bought most of my merchandise directly from the manufacturer. We dealt in big quantities. Here your main trouble is overbuying—buying too long a line or too many lines. You keep thinking you must carry a wide variety of lines. This is true to a great extent if you are in a big store, but too many items you think will sell, don't. Then what? It means disposing of obsolete stock at a sale, and there go your profits.

After a number of years, I realized that my mistakes in buying incorrectly were in my unfamiliarity with the demands of the customers. I didn't spend enough time on the selling floor. Yet, I didn't have the time to wander out on the floor and tend to my buying, too.

Buying committees pay off

That's when I selected a buying committee to assist me and this turned out to be one of my most intelligent moves. I set up a committee of three—my immediate assistant, my best "volume" salesman and my top salesman in the appreciation of styling. If we had women on the floor, I would select my best "volume" sales person from among them for they not only could sell but also understood style and customer appeals.

Many items that I thought were a cinch to sell were rejected by my committee. I respected their judgment and made them partners in my efforts. Some buyers figure they are too important to consult their salesmen, or they think they should not be influenced by any judgments but their own. I disagree.

My partnership with my committee was one of my most important steps to effective buying.

A committee, such as I formed, proved of considerable help when

a salesman confronted me with a discontinued item that he claimed was a sure seller. I'd invite my committee to look over the sample and join me in listening to the salesman's pitch. When he was through, I'd ask him to step out of the office and I would then invite my committee to vote. How many should we buy, at what cost, and what should be our selling price?

When I compared notes, I was always amazed at the consistency in their thinking. If the vendor offered us 200 of the item and the committee agreed on, let's say, 150, I often gambled on the other 50, thereby taking the whole closeout and controlling its price and distribution in my area. Sometimes, if the quantity was larger, the source of supply would be willing to hold the remainder for later purchase. That's where friendly relationships come in handy.

I also noticed that when I consulted the committee and its members participated in a purchase, each worked harder to sell that item in order to prove his judgment had been right. They had become better acquainted with the buying problem.

Don't forget your sales staff

I would also enlist the help of my sales staff in keeping tabs on the competition. Every buyer must know what his competition is doing. Customers have a habit of exaggerating lower prices they claim prevail at another store. I'd assign one of my staff to sample the product, to make sure it was the same as we had and that the price was truly lower. Sometimes the competition conducted a quick sale and the product was available at a lower price only for a limited time. It's easy to give away profits if you listen to your customers without first checking on their claims. We were always careful to meet prices only when we knew we were honestly being undersold.

Visiting our competition helped in another way, too. We often learned of a new display, a dramatic promotion or—believe it or not—a price increase by competition. We'd hop right on these ideas, if they were good, and adapt them to our store.

By the same token, I made it a point to visit my resources whenever possible, especially those in my own area. I'd never pass up an "open house." I'd always wander through the warehouse. You can often come up with an idea for a deal. Maybe there'd be a certain number of a line in stock and you might be able to buy the entire lot at a price; or you might be able to talk the boss into giving you something you need badly which he might have shipped elsewhere.

If nothing else, you can acquaint yourself with lines you are not stocking. In case some customer questions you about such an item you will know where to turn in a hurry. A buyer must continually study the market—not only the items he buys but those he doesn't.

Such visits might enable a buyer to test run some item or line. Being on good terms with your suppliers makes such experiments possible.

Know what's new

There are two other ways to keep up with the market—with what's new. The first is your trade publications; the second is the catalogs of jobbers and manufacturers. Build up a library of these books and don't hesitate to consult them.

Personally, in the hard goods field, I always read *Home Furnishings Daily;* in sporting goods, it was *The Sporting Goods Dealer* magazine. They were my "bibles," I couldn't do without them. They tipped me off on the Chicago and New York market trends. They told me what was new and described promotional ideas that were clicking. I'd learn of model changes and would be aware of the latest on the market long before the competition. Never be too busy to read your leading trade papers. There is gold between their pages.

These short cuts to better buying bear repeating:

(1) Establish a pleasant relationship with your salesman and your supplier.

(2) Stress quality first, then price.

(3) Develop a partnership with your key salespeople.

(4) Check your competition on prices and promotions.

(5) Keep in close touch with your nearby suppliers.

(6) Never be too busy to read your trade magazines.

Chapter 3. The new buyer takes over . . . now what?

There is nothing more frustrating than moving into a new position for which you've actually had no specific, advance training. Oh, yes, I know that most men who are promoted are generally capable of taking over, otherwise they wouldn't have been elevated. This is as true for buyers as it is for merchandise managers or others.

What I mean, though, is that they seldom have tasted the responsibility that suddenly is thrust upon their shoulders. Maybe the buyer works with his successor-to-be a week before the changeover, or maybe even a month. So what? It isn't enough.

It's worse if the retiring buyer was the kind who kept most of his records in his head. Or in his secretary's head.

So you're the new buyer and the din of all the congratulations has died down. Now what? Where do you start?

Check your warehouse

The first thing would be to visit the warehouse, or if it is a smaller store, go back into the stockroom and live there, for a few days if necessary, going over the stock from top to bottom. If your employer, or the buyer before you, has provided you with some inventory figures, take them along. Study the figures, but don't trust them. Check them against the actual stock and make sure just what you have on hand.

Become familiar with every item you carry—how many, model numbers, stock numbers, any and all other identifying marks. Take notes. Visualize what you have so that you can see almost everything even when you are back at your desk or at home.

When this is completed, think back. How did you find the stock?

Was it neatly arranged? Did you have trouble locating items? Was everything easily accessible? If not, make it a point to correct any such weakness. If you can't find it, the next fellow will have just as much trouble. This means a loss of time and you should lick that right at the beginning.

Next, check your inventory. I mean the items on the sales floor. You have become acquainted with your stockroom or warehouse, now what have you on the counters and on the shelves? Double check this with the listing provided when you took over. Make sure it is right.

As you check inventory—and I urge that it be a workable perpetual inventory—look at all the items closely. Are they displayed to best advantage? Is everything clean? Are all items good items? Are they moving? Take notes along the route. Also consult your salespeople. What do they think of some of the articles? Would they rather see a better grade or a better price? Have them help you "feel" the value of the merchandise.

Work on office files

Now that you are familiar with your warehouse and your on-floor inventory, start working on your office files. Take material home with you for a few nights. Read what's gone on before. What were some of the complaints? How were they handled? With whom was the previous buyer friendly? Why? Become better acquainted with your suppliers through previous correspondence. Look at their literature and brochures, which should be in the files.

If you have trouble locating all this, maybe you should revamp the filing system. Go ahead. A filing system is only good if you and others working with you can easily understand it.

If the files don't produce a complete list of all resources and their contacts, make an alphabetical list of your own—the name of the person to contact, phone number and address. Prepare a list that will enable you to make a quick phone call to the right person at the right time without wasted effort. Phone numbers are a buyer's best friends.

Know your assistants

All this accomplished? Okay. Now get to know your assistants, if any, and your salespeople. Their personalities are different and it is up to you to find out where they differ. These people mean your future. Be friendly, be fair, be interested.

I know that business is supposedly getting colder these days. All

cut and dried and loaded with statistics. Much of that is good, but people are still as human today as they were fifty years ago.
You take the cold facts and figures; I'll take a spirited, cooperative team of salespeople and I'll outsell you day to day.

Most buyers are required to assist in the preparation of advertising or they have to do it all. This is another reason why all your resources and their literature should be handy at all times.
Good advertising depends on complete information about the products. Your files should provide this quickly.

Some buyers shudder at the thought of preparing an advertisement. They insist they are not advertisers, they are buyers. Don't kid yourself. If you're a good buyer, you are automatically the best bet for writing the best copy. You know the product better than anyone else, or at least you should. Just put yourself into the shoes of the potential customer. Why should he come to your store and buy your product? Why are you so enthusiastic about it? What's so good about it? Is it a special bargain, a special quality, or an exclusive?

Somewhere your office should be able to tell you how much was spent on advertising last year and even the year before that.
You should be able to find out what articles were featured and you should be able to obtain all the rates—newspaper, radio and television. You should also have available to you (if you don't, be sure and get this right away) any arrangements with your suppliers on previous advertising allowances. By all means, keep close records on advertising expenditures.

Keep *an* advertising scrapbook

I always kept a big advertising scrapbook. I placed all ads in this book, by departments. I would jot down beside the ad the amount of business it brought in, plus other comments on why it was a good or weak ad. Include your cost, the retail price and your profits. This is necessary for the best results in future advertising.

"Yes, but when does the buyer actually get enough time to buy?" you may ask impatiently.

That comes quicker than you think and if you're prepared, you're in position to do a good job. In buying, you again consult your records. How much was bought last year? From whom? In what quantities and what periods of shipment? You should keep each resource separate, including a complete record of transactions, with invoices. Also know your quota, if your store provides one.

Then comes the judgment play based on your records, on your

current inventory and your own glance into the crystal ball. How much should you buy now? Don't be afraid to play your hunches if you've been fortified with the proper records. However, if you haven't had a chance to check your warehouse, your inventory, your own people and your files—don't gamble. Take it easy. Tell the salesman, in all honesty, that you aren't yet prepared. You might place a fill-in order, but don't let him rush you into anything drastic. Maybe he'll gamble with you. Many do. That's okay, but don't take any plunge until you've felt the water. It would be sure death if the tank were dry as you were coming off the diving board.

Simple?

Maybe, but so many buyers are flustered their first few days that they forget to take things one at a time and never do settle down, even after fifty years. I plead with you to be calm. Don't let them pull you in every direction at once. Do first things first and do them thoroughly. Move from one step to the other until you're ready to run, then you'll be on the way to the top.

Chapter 4. Putting the "show" in showmanship

Sometimes showmanship is misconstrued to mean ballyhoo—the knack of promoting something with only a minor value. I'm of the old school and believe showmanship means just what it says—the ability to "show" a product to the best and most dramatic advantage.

Showmanship is not reserved for the seller. The buyer must also recognize its value and be alert to it. It isn't enough to merely buy some merchandise; you must help your salespeople dispose of your inventory. This I practiced with reckless abandon and never hesitated to solicit the cooperation of my resources.

I particularly stressed clinics, exhibits, special displays and good old-fashioned shows. Some were staged on the sales floor, others in the auditorium available in my store. Now I know some buyers work for smaller companies, yet there is always a nearby auditorium you can rent, either in a school, club, hotel or some municipal arena.

Among the events I promoted annually was a camera show. Another was my popular pet show. While in sporting goods I presented fishing and hunting demonstrations. My music carnival was sure-fire in my radio-TV-record department.

Have suppliers man booths

In my shows, I would line the auditorium walls with various booths, inviting my suppliers to man these. I know that some manufacturers frown on such activities because they often tie up their men who should be on the road. However, if yours is a well-planned sales getter, factories are always ready to cooperate. They will compete to be invited. It's up to you to make it worth their time and expense.

Our shows encouraged question and answer periods and plenty

of demonstrations. My camera show would cover a three-day period with selling right on the exhibit floor, aided by our sales staff. We'd have good-looking models on hand to take pictures. The good will of these shows extended for weeks afterward. Crowds jammed the place, thanks to organized, advance billing by our advertising department. A buyer needs cooperation and help from all sides in a venture such as this.

Pet shows pull

One of our best attractions was the pet show. We encouraged the mighty and the mongrels, the puppies and the older dogs to participate. The center of the floor was transformed into a fenced-in arena and the public was permitted a close look. Dog fanciers, trainers and many others would welcome an opportunity to step into the arena and strut their dogs, cats, birds, and even hamsters.

The local obedience clubs would be on hand several times to demonstrate animal obedience. This always is a crowd puller.

The poodle people would rush to parade their French poodles. We'd show what the well-dressed poodles were wearing, some in mink jackets, little hats, red roses. Then we'd dress them in a rain outfit, boots, hat and raincoat, carrying a little umbrella. The public would scream—and with each scream we were making a new friend for the store.

There would also be myna birds that talked. And parrots, parakeets and lovebirds were especially attractive to youngsters who would flock to the store after school. We'd even have a veterinarian standing by to take care of accidents and answer questions of the pet lovers.

Sporting goods is a natural for shows, especially demonstrations. We'd get a local field and stream editor, for example, to tell about the best fishing spots, hotel and camping accommodations and equipment for vacation fishing trips. We'd even publish maps of certain angling areas and give these away. They'd tell where to stop, where to catch fish and with what. For camping fans, we'd set up tents complete with all equipment.

To demonstrate insulated underwear which has become popular in recent years, we'd have one of our chief suppliers send a man to the store to spend hours in a cake of ice. This would prove conclusively that the underwear he was wearing was insulated against cold. Crowds would stand around him and ask questions. Some sympathetic women would even bring him coffee.

Three ring circus

I'll never forget the three-ring circus I once tried some years back. This event was even too big for our auditorium so we used part of the sporting goods department on the eighth floor as well. Included were a six-day bike race on a treadmill, wrestling matches starring the champion of St. Louis, and exhibition dives into an enormous canvas tank. The tank was so big we cracked the ceiling for extra space and the diver would plunge 35 feet through this hole into a tank filled with water.

One night the tank sprung a leak. They reached me at my home about 2 A.M. and I rushed to the store. The floor was flooded and not a drop was left in the tank. Thanks to a lot of hard work by every one concerned we relined the tank with metal, cleaned up the place and all was in readiness for the first show the next day.

More people attended this show than any other. At times the crowds were so big we couldn't sell. However, here again, customers kept coming in for weeks later on the strength of this show. We staged many swimming shows after that, some with attractive gals as well as divers. They always clicked.

Putting the "show" in showmanship is important for every buyer. People flock to see the dramatic—and if you have the right product, such interest spells sales as well.

Chapter 5. Private brand for extra profits

Keener competition from discount houses, chain stores and even supermarkets is placing new values on private brand merchandise. As you know, a private brand line is one that is tailored to the tastes of the buyer and carried exclusively by his company. It competes with nationally advertised merchandise.

I happen to be a buyer who is convinced that private brands are an excellent antidote to price-cut competition.

But I warn other buyers to investigate this possibility carefully before coming to any decision. Adding a private brand is something of great importance.

Get the right supplier

The first step is to find the proper resource or supplier. You should be well prepared and know exactly what you have in mind, what you want of your resource. Consult your assistants and your sales staff, if you have such help. Try to assemble as much information and as many opinions as possible. Know what your customers have been seeking from day to day. Remember the better qualities of the nationally advertised brand and add some ideas of your own. What styles or models are popular? What price will sell? If it's a television set or a record player, for example, what colors and finishes are preferred? What features of convenience have the most appeal? Just what do your customers desire?

Next, you must look for the right resource which isn't always the simplest task. You'll need someone who can meet all your requirements for the product you have in mind. You'll want a supplier with a good reputation and one who will carry out his delivery promises. Check the financial status of the company. Most of all. will this firm be willing to play along with your ideas and at the right price so that you can be assured of a fair profit?

Loyalty pays off

When you find this resource, be loyal to it. Don't flirt with other companies or pit one against the other in a bidding war.
Don't probe others to see what they might have done. You're wasting valuable time and money. It'll take a while to develop your brand to what you want, so stay with one company.

It's important to remember that quality is a vital factor in the success of a private brand. Chances are you decided to seek a private brand in the first place because of price. You wanted to beat your competition in price. Well, it's a funny reaction that customers have. Though they shop for price, if you offer them a private brand at a lower price, they then suspect its quality. They'll insist on your proving that the quality matches the national brand most desired. Your product must include many of the features of your number one competition, plus a few of your own—and at a better price.

You can't just sell price. Remember that.

Once your private brand meets this test, your repeat business will amaze you. They'll keep coming back for this item and many more. They have a greater trust in your name than in some well known brand whose origin is far from their home city. In most instances, your own personal name and that of your store is closer to the customer than any national brand. People like to trade
with someone they know and trust.

Original ideas incorporated in your private brand item mean extra business for you since all this enables your salesman to
say, "Here's something you won't find in any other make."

Restrict your selection

Select only one or two models in a line until you know just where you stand. Be sure they're in competitive price ranges, aimed at your competition's strongest suit.

Of course, local promotion is more important to a private brand than to a nationally known product. You have to develop your own advertising and acceptance and you must be certain to have money in your budget to do that. Obviously, it takes more work to introduce a private brand than a national one. For that reason, I've displayed my private brands more prominently than others. I wanted my customers to see my brand first, and I provided our sales staff with extra incentives to push it.

Big mail-order houses and chains have proved, down through

the years, that private brands can assume a rightful role in merchandising if they are properly promoted, properly priced, properly advertised and properly displayed.

I know, in my own case, private brands always exceeded my fondest expectations.

Chapter 6. Speeding up slow-moving merchandise

The password for the successful buyer is "perpetual inventory." If the buyer is not aware of what he has on hand, he's in trouble. He'll be either overbuying or underselling.

Oh, you know what you have because the office gives you a monthly accounting. Well, you're kidding yourself. A monthly inventory isn't enough, not even a weekly report. A perpetual inventory is the only answer. If you have an assistant, that's the job for him. It's his best training.

I always knew the condition of my stock at one glance. No item was too small to be inventoried. This kept all of us on our toes.

Old merchandise is the bugaboo of the trade. It has three main faults:

1. It keeps profits down.

2. It stifles the buying of new merchandise.

3. It clutters the floor and the shelves, taking up precious space.

Buyer's responsibility

The blame of old merchandise rests on the shoulders of the buyer. He simply wasn't careful. He bought too many models or too many-styles within one model. Also he didn't push hard enough for sales when the goods were new.

It doesn't take long nor does it require special talents to realize when the public has stopped buying a certain item. We all know the moment a product has begun to lag in sales, but we try to deny it. We think maybe tomorrow it'll start moving. I'll let you in on a little secret—there never is a tomorrow. Each day you fail to take cognizance of this situation, the stock grows older and moving it is that much tougher.

As soon as you feel an item has stopped selling, check your inventory and your budget. They'll let you know what your next move can be.

I red-tagged all old merchandise on the floor, a reminder to salespeople that extra effort should be made to clear out the item. Also, I often arranged for better commissions on it. Your budget will tell you if you can afford this. You must get rid of the stock, and the sooner the better.

At my weekly meetings with the sales staff, I always stressed moving old merchandise. They all understood how old merchandise prevented us from obtaining and selling new lines.

Group old merchandise

Often I would group old merchandise in one corner of the department or, if it was of a smaller variety, I'd set aside a special counter and let the public know we were trying to close it out. There's no reason to be coy about such matters.

Whenever you buy. picture what you will do if that item stops moving. How will you get rid of it? Can you afford some more old merchandise? Your perpetual inventory will provide the answers.

Suppliers have the same problems and they'll come to you with a good buy on old or discontinued merchandise. Should you buy? Or should you skip it? Look at your perpetual inventory. It'll help you make up your mind.

Whenever I was low on my budget, I would buy only to cover a sale, even if I sold the sample on the floor. I'd resort to the catalog, if necessary, to sell a customer.

Spot your old merchandise quickly and speed up the sale of slow movers.

Chapter 7. Promotions spell p-r-o-f-i-t

With the Federal government turning a jaundiced eye toward price comparisons in advertising, especially where the larger stores are involved, greater attention must be paid to promotions. I've always been an ardent promotion enthusiast. I could become so excited over a new item that I'd be thinking up a dozen or more ways to promote it—some solid, some silly.

A successful buyer not only must be an ace salesman—knowing as soon as he sees a new line whether he could sell it—but he also must be able to conjure up promotional ideas right on the spot. He must be able to visualize this merchandise in an advertisement and on his sales floor. What's he going to do to drum up as much interest among customers as he himself has? Of course, he's sold on it. Now how will he sell his prospects?

I'll admit I was a pretty good "price" man in advertising, but as the years went by I became just as adept at extolling the features of the merchandise and, later, the promotional values.

Omnibus newspaper ads

I was one of the first who favored the omnibus type of newspaper advertisements. There'd be a smashing, powerful headline over the whole ad and then maybe from five to twenty-five boxes devoted to special items. Copy would range from fifty to two hundred lines. Each box told a different story for a different item.

Maybe I'd feature the best seller in each make of radio that I handled, one box for each. If I decided to promote television, I might select one major line and then show various models in the ads, one box to each model. Or I'd play up the different stylings and finishes.

If I were advertising during the hunting season, I would have a box for various guns, clothing, decoys, scopes and one each for other

accessories. I would handle cameras the same way, showing a series within a line or best sellers in various lines.

Yes, price would be important but, more than that, this type of promotion focuses the reader's attention on the many items carried within a department or within a line; it shows you have a variety of price ranges—low, medium and high. Your higher prices make your lower prices seem even lower, yet you are not cutting price or comparing with other stores.

Also, if you show enough items within one ad you'll increase your telephone and mail-order business. We always did well with telephone and mail orders the day after an omnibus ad. People could find exactly what they wanted without entering the store.

Prestige ads

Of course, I also prepared many prestige ads and, when I did, I'd select one outstanding model and give it 250 to 500 lines and sometimes a full page. I'd make sure the illustration was the best and in a setting that would tempt the reader. Not just a television set, for example, but a television set in the living room of a home.

If I were introducing an exclusive line or a private brand, I would go all out with a special advertisement—one that would combine quality with attractiveness.

Equally as important as advertising is on-floor display. No matter how good an item may be, floor display must never be overlooked. Always put your best foot forward. Many times, the distributor or the manufacturer will be happy to provide special display material. Take advantage of this. If you're featuring private brand lines, supervise the display yourself. I'd always put my private brands up front in a choice position.

Build atmosphere wherever possible. If you're showing a television set, make it homelike with furniture and draperies nearby— at least for the model on which you are placing greatest emphasis. If you merely line up a string of models, it will be price that attracts attention, certainly not the sets themselves.

If you're showing a record player, for example, have some popular hit records close at hand for added atmosphere and for the customer to play. The music itself may sell him.

All of this also holds true when designing a window display.

The emphasis of the better stores is away from price cutting, what with government pressure and the lack of profit in price slashing. So it's up to the buyer to keep promotions in mind as he conducts the continual search for better profits.

Chapter 8. How to buy and then sell close-outs

In my many years as buyer I bought out inventories of hundreds of stores which were going out of business or of manufacturers who were offering close-outs of entire lines. No matter what size store you represent, close-out opportunities are always around you. Don't be afraid to plunge, but stay within your means.

Walk down your main street from time to time and step into some of your neighborhood shopping centers. Do you see any stores that look as if they might be in trouble? Are any stores conducting a going-out-of-business sale and not doing well? Make some inquiries and you'll be surprised at the opportunities available for a good buy.

Buy it all

Whatever you do, buy the entire lot. Only if you buy it all will you have complete jurisdiction over disposition of the stock—and this is very important. It means you can set the time for the sale and the price.

The proper timing of such sales is the key to a profitable deal. I am a firm believer in holding such merchandise until the spring or early summer. Business usually picks up in the fall, which eliminates that as a good time for close-out promotion. November and December are peak months because of Christmas, so why hold a sale then? January and February generally are slow months and not even a sale will pick them up. March and April are doubtful and at Easter it's best not to think of any special sale. This leaves May, June and July as the best months.

Naturally much depends on the size of your purchase. If it is only a small stock, you might conduct the sale shortly after the purchase. But if it is sizable, or seasonal, hold up until the right time.

My biggest deal

How did I handle a big close-out deal?

Let's recall my biggest deal of all—the purchase of the inventory of the bankrupt Dowd Sporting Goods Company in St. Louis in 1950. Here was a fine store with a heavy inventory and a court order to liquidate. I became interested and had my staff study the inventory and help determine its value. It was called a $500,000 stock at retail prices. We bid $145,000.

There were other bidders and we weren't the highest, but the court favored us because it knew our store would sell this stock all at one time and would not prolong the event for months or come back repeatedly with other sales based on parts of this stock.
Some stores conduct a sale for weeks upon weeks, adding to the stock whenever it gets low. This the court wished to discourage.

We moved the stock to our warehouse. It was late spring and I decided we would hold the big sale early in summer, since much of the stock was warm weather sports merchandise. We marked the merchandise and checked it against our own stock. We surveyed the items and, as is true of many such purchases, were confronted with our share of junk.

Clean out junk

Now I'm one who insists on cleaning out junk. To do this we called in secondhand men or others who might be interested and sold the merchandise for whatever we could get. We didn't wait for any sale. I followed this procedure for two reasons. First, we never wanted to take up valuable counter space with such merchandise; second, to keep junk around gives customers the idea the whole lot is not up to par.

I'd also look over such lots for merchandise we didn't normally sell and, even if it was pretty good, I'd try and peddle it before the sale opened. For example, we didn't sell schools any athletic equipment such as tape, liniments, shoe strings and the like. Consequently, I contacted local schools and other interested parties and sold all such Dowd goods to them in advance. We also did not deal in trophies. Now this is a good item, but it never had fitted into our scheme of selling; so rather than begin to learn about trophies (which aren't good items for such sales), I sold all of them to another store, getting just about what I paid for them.

We called our sales staff to the warehouse and began pricing the

Dowd stock. We'd ask one of our men what a certain article was worth. If it was $1.00, we'd ask him how much we might get for it. If he said 49 cents, that's what it would be. Since you usually pick up these close-out lots for about 20 to 30 cents on a dollar and, since we usually figure on making 35 per cent, we could easily sell this merchandise for 50 to 60 per cent off regular prices and still come out ahead.

Use first floor space

In the case of this Dowd stock, we moved it to the store in time for our big sale, taking over the entire floor. We even used choice space on the first floor to attract general customers. This is a point to keep in mind. Conduct your sale in a special spot. If the stock isn't too big, place it in the front of the store if yours is a smaller shop. If you are in a multifloor store, be sure you obtain at least a corner on the first floor for added promotional value.

We announced the sale in the newspapers and then management began making bets as to how much we'd move the first day. Most optimistic guess was $20,000. I hoped for $30,000. We hit $50,000 that first day. It was a madhouse. We had about one hundred clerks where we usually had fifteen.

The reason? The store from which this stock came was well known and our firm was dependable. People knew that when we conducted a sale it was truly a sale with no gimmick to kid customers along. We had planned well and it was a success from the start. It lasted only about nine days. We still had some merchandise left, but cleaned it out on special deals and incorporated some of it in our own inventory.

Know when to stop

This brings up another factor to remember. End the sale when interest begins to lag. Don't drag it out. Know when to quit.

I've also picked up many smaller stocks. I remember, for instance, buying out a record shop for $1,300. This was a good offer— the best the young fellow had. Also, it was the third time I had bought him out. He was always starting up a small business, then swinging into something else.

When I do something like this I send my crew of markers to that store to price the merchandise right on the scene. This is much easier than packing it, unpacking later at the warehouse and then marking and pricing it.

We set up a separate bay for these records, away from our record

department. I was always averse to mingling close-out merchandise with my own, even if some numbers were alike. A sale is a sale so don't chisel by switching around merchandise. We tried self-service whenever possible since sales such as this sell themselves. And you must keep down costs. In three days we were down low enough to quit. I then put some of the leftovers in with my other stock, raised the prices and that ended the sale. If I had conducted this sale within my department, when would I have been able to go back to my regular prices?

Watch out for part-time help on such occasions. When we staged the Dowd sale, we also hired special clerks who were familiar with the merchandise. Imagine my chagrin when our security men uncovered a plot to clean us out of valuable fishing tackle. Unknown to me, some of the clerks were working in league with customers, selling 99 cent tackle boxes with hundreds of dollars of reels and baits inside. The ring was broken up within twenty-four hours. Let this be a lesson to you. Be most careful of your personnel during any big sale. Double your security forces.

Close-outs can open up added profits for you. Keep your eyes open for them.

Chapter 9. Chalking up record sales with a recorder

"Tall oaks from little acorns grow" is an old adage, I know, but this holds a more significant meaning to me now that I can look back on my experience with a tape recorder.

It started the morning the president of an importing firm phoned to ask why I had not reordered on his bicycles. I had purchased several hundred and much to my chagrin they weren't moving as anticipated. The price was right, but they weren't catching on with our sales staff or with the public.

This surprised him even more than it did me, for they were selling well in other department stores. He requested an opportunity to come up and talk the whole matter over with me. I welcomed the idea.

A few days later he came to the store, looked at the stock and then sat down in my office. He started to relate some key selling points to me, and did so with enthusiasm. He was making a lot of sense.

Know features of merchandise

One particular advantage of his bike occurred to me—the control of the coaster brake was in the handle, not in the foot pedal.

I certainly wasn't aware of this point and wondered if my salespeople knew of it. I checked and, sure enough, they hadn't given this any consideration either.

The fellow huddled with the clerks for a few moments and demonstrated this important advantage. The clerks became excited over it and couldn't wait to tell the first customer who asked about a

bike. What's more, the bikes began selling and we cleared out the couple of hundred quickly and I reordered.

I suddenly woke up to an idea.

"If only this man could give that same sales pitch to my people in our branch stores, they'd start selling more of his bikes." I convinced myself I was on the track of something worthwhile. Since he didn't have time to make the rounds, maybe I could arrange to have his voice and sales talk make the circuit instead.

I invited him to repeat his sales pitch and recorded it as he talked. He warmed up to the idea, too, and gave it everything he had. I sent the tape to our outlying stores and the results were astounding. Our sales soared.

I began putting the tape recorder to extensive use as other sales managers, sales representatives or company executives came into my office. I had them all record their messages and we'd play them back at sales meetings. It worked.

Record good sales talks

Also, when I found one of our staff doing an especially good job in selling a certain item, I would have this person record his sales talk. We'd try out different sales approaches on new items, permitting each clerk to record his suggestions and then we'd sit around and criticize—constructively and good naturedly. The clerks soon began to enjoy this. They listened carefully to their own voices and even corrected their enunciation. The stunt improved their manner of speaking.

But the best idea of all was my use of the recorder to sell recorders.

It was a funny thing, but we weren't selling many recorders. We tried them in our record department, but no luck. Then we tried them in the camera department and this didn't work any better.

So I called the sales manager of one of the companies and asked him to record his best sales points on the recorder he was trying to sell. He felt awkward at first, but then accepted the challenge. He described in detail the major aspects of his recorder and why it was well worth the price. We played this back to the sales staff, they discussed all the angles, they became enthused and we had no trouble selling recorders after that in either department.

The sales manager went a step further. He agreed to explain the recorder not only to our sales staff but to some customers who had purchased one recently. We sent him to their homes or offices and

had him demonstrate the recorder, making sure they were getting maximum use out of it. The customers were much impressed with the service we were providing and with the extra help they received from the sales manager.

Word soon made the rounds that we were interested in our customers after a sale as well as before.

I also began using the recorder more myself. I'd tape suggestions and listen to myself. It prepared me just that much more for my sales meetings.

Yes, the tape recorder began setting new sales records for me.

Chapter 10. This little buyer went to market

Going to the market can be an exciting thing, especially if it is a first. The buyer should take his assistant along. Usually the assistant has to stay at home and "mind the store," but if you have your people well trained they can man the ship for the few days you both are away. The advantages to your assistant are invaluable.

In preparing to go to the market I usually set up a schedule. I'd get a budget so I would know how much money I could spend and then I would allocate it to the specific items. I would review the market and visit resources. I would listen to all the close-out offers. By this time I would be able to look at my budget and know just where I was going to put my money.

Now, when you have your assistant with you, you have a little more responsibility. Let's say it's his first time. He'll need to be introduced to representatives of the various firms exhibiting and to the men with whom you are working. Let him make a note of those with whom you do business.

Train your assistant

If he's worth making a buyer out of, he's worth training. And what better way than right here where you do your sharpest buying. Many times when you aren't around or it isn't convenient for you to take a long-distance call, he will be able to relieve you. Sometimes you want him to be in on the phone conversation. Those very things happened to me many times and it's always worked like a charm.

In visiting the market I always made it a practice to visit every display, whether I carried the item or not. Many times I would run into something that was unusual but would fit in with my program. By concentrating on the item and with proper promotion I'd sell thousands. So I always had an open mind.

Sometimes, too, the firms would have items hidden away and I'd ask them whether they were ashamed to let the public see their wares. They'd take the hint and bring them out. Many times I would buy the item in quantity and have a successful event by asking silly questions.

Having your assistant along sometimes gives you a different slant on an item. He's closer to the public and his judgment on the potential is at times better than yours.

Usually the firms exhibiting have special private rooms where they ask you to sit down and discuss your problems in detail, away from the noise and confusion of the national show. It is generally in these rooms where the majority of the deals are made and close-outs and discontinued numbers are discussed.

Visit manufacturers' plants

Then, too, many exhibitors have their plants in the city where the show is being held and you are invited there. This is always a profitable expedition, not only to see for yourself the type of firm it is, but also to note its size and equipment.

I recall an incident when I went to the market with my merchandise man. He was quite a prominent figure in the store and was a great producer. He had a sort of sixth sense when it came to buying. This particular time we called at the plant of one of our resources. Usually, we got an inventory or estimate of what was offered, but not him. He sized up one side of the wall where the shelves were loaded and also those items which were on the floor. He gave his offer without bothering to see what else was in the place. He nearly always got what he wanted at his terms. It used to look to me as if he was stealing the deal but his eyes were so well trained and he was so sharp that he could tell in an instant the value of stock. I wouldn't recommend that type of buying; in fact, that wouldn't do today at all.

I remember one time, too, this same merchandise man, the general merchandise man and I were working on an inventory of some merchandise I had bought. It was out of line and he bawled me out for having bought so much and so unwisely. I thought that I was going to get fired. But the general merchandise man turned to him and said, "If you hadn't countersigned the orders he wouldn't have gotten the merchandise." So it was a lesson for both of us.

Learn to gamble

Here is where your assistant will learn one of the cardinal points of buying, You have to learn how to gamble a little and you have to

know instinctively when a close-out is right for you, at what cost you can sell it for the greatest profit, and what discontinued models you can move. You have to decide, too, how much to buy and, if there is a limited quantity, whether to buy the lot.

While you are buying close-outs and making deals you always have to remember your basic stock; that you have to keep a certain amount of staples. You have to keep your eye on the "overloading" end of it and have to stay within your budget. When I get to the end of my budget I buy as I sell.

Whatever you buy at the market you will have to give orders to cover. There you must have an understanding as to cost, terms, time of delivery, warranties, the quantity you are buying immediately and what will be held for future orders.

It is so important to know how much to buy. If there is any doubt in your mind about the selling potential of an item, it is best to sample it and then reorder. Sometimes I would special order merchandise until I was satisfied of the customer demand. When you see the public likes it, then don't wait until you're entirely sold out before reordering.

Chapter 11. My miracle sales chart

Developing an incentive among salesclerks is most important in the sale of merchandise. Competition, of course, is one way in which to boost the desire to sell more. Cash rewards are a natural, but one can't forever keep paying extra for added productivity. A successful buyer is one who receives the most cooperation from his salesclerks.

I had been a buyer for almost fifty years before my best idea for incentives without added pay was born; it was so simple, based on so old an idea, you'd hardly believe it possible.

Any department, or any store for that matter, is confronted with a number of sales hurdles, among which is the problem of moving old, even obsolete, merchandise; another is emphasis on private brands where profit is higher. How can you drum up enthusiasm among your clerks in these important phases of selling?

"Gold star" reward

It was only a few years ago that I found the answer—my miracle chart. It was merely a large sheet of signboard, divided into sections for each salesperson. Next to each name was a row of gold stars. Yes, gold stars—an old grade-school trick of distinguishing the best student.

I hit upon this idea one day after watching the salespeople taking the least line of resistance, that is, selling new merchandise and permitting old stock to pile up. Why not place a gold star after the names of those most willing to do a little extra to induce customers to buy the older items? That's when my chart was born.

This idea turned out to be excellent for another simple reason: it enlisted the support of salespeople in a department's progress giving them a chance to understand and participate in a department's goal.

I called my salespeople together and explained my idea. All those who sold old merchandise would be given a gold star; those who moved private brand lines would receive a red star; those who sold only new articles—well, they'd get no stars for that wasn't the purpose of my miracle chart.

What would they get in return?

"No extra money except the usual commissions, of course," I declared. "However," I emphasized, "by helping to clean out the old, the sales staff will be making it possible for the buyer to acquire new stock, including some fast sellers; for the more money the buyer has, the better his chance of supplying the right merchandise for his salespeople. When the new merchandise arrives, it will be easy selling for the clerks and that means more commissions."

As for private brands, the clerks were made to realize that selling these meant extra profit for the department, which again would assist the buyer in obtaining new and better lines.

I showed them the chart with their names and told them to go to it.

Old merchandise moved fast

You'd be surprised at the splendid reaction. They began to worry about the stars after their names. We moved more old merchandise than ever before and they grew prouder and prouder of their achievement. They had begun to understand the mechanics of a closer relationship between buyer and salesclerks.

When members of top management visited my offices they always went over and studied the chart. They were amazed at its simpleness and its effectiveness. They became acquainted with some of the top producers and would go out and congratulate them. This was an unanticipated by-product of the chart, the chance for recognition of leading salesmen by top management.

The psychological effect of this chart on the department went far beyond expectations. Not only that, but top management soon duplicated the idea in other departments.

Yes, sometimes the oldest ideas often are the best. Don't be afraid to try something, even if it does sound a bit childish; after all, we're all still kids at heart.

Chapter 12. Mistakes you can easily avoid

Everybody makes mistakes, they say, but it's a funny thing that mine always seemed to catch up with me. There is no reason for making mistakes when you can fall back on someone else's experiences, so I'll let you in on some of mine.

A buyer must overcome the temptation to tantalize the salesman who calls on him. Many buyers are under the impression that some of the salesmen may be making more money than they, so they torture them a bit. After all, a buyer figures, this fellow is going to make a lot of money on my order, why shouldn't he sweat a little?

I admit I followed this tendency in my earlier days; maybe not because I thought I was making less, but because I didn't want them to make their commissions without some worry; make them earn it, so to speak.

Rudeness is inexcusable

I'd let some of them sit outside my office too long. Many times they were in town only for a day, and my inexcusable action forced them to stay over. On occasion, when a manufacturer's representative or a salesman telephoned long distance, I would keep him waiting awhile before answering.

Oh, I'd get away with it from time to time, but soon I began to lose business. Some salesmen would simply get up and walk away if they were kept waiting too long. Or they'd hang up before I answered the phone.

The result? The loss of a chance for a good buy.

I recall the time I was a young buyer at Rothschild's in Chicago. A salesman called on me one day, claiming he had a hit item. I suggested he sit on the bench outside my door and wait. I thought this would impress him with my importance.

As I went out to lunch, he stopped me and asked if he could

see me before I headed for the restaurant. I shook him off and said I'd talk to him afterward. I came back late, hurried into my office and paid no attention to him. He finally left and I forgot the incident. After all, who was I to worry about some kid salesman?

A couple of days later one of our competitors came out with a big newspaper advertisement, heralding the product this fellow was trying to sell me. It was a big hit and my boss called me into his office to find out what happened. I admitted my "poor judgment." I had learned my lesson.

As I grew older and as some of these cases of inexperience and rudeness backfired, I changed my habits. Let me tell you, the salesman who calls on you can be and should be your best friend. Treat him with the respect and courtesy he deserves. Have an open-door policy. Encourage them to make appointments in advance, but if they do drop in unannounced, take it with a smile and give them a few moments. If you need more time, suggest they call back. Let them know it was really their fault, not yours, that you couldn't spend more time with them at that particular moment; but do it gracefully.

Don't be too smart

Another mistake too many buyers are guilty of is to make all the decisions themselves. You begin to believe you are smarter than anybody else. The smartest move I made was to consult with my best salespeople. Whenever I was ready for a big buy, the purchase of a close-out, for example, I'd consult my buying committee. If they were skeptical of the deal, I'd check into it further. After all, you must have their support if it is to sell. Sometimes it is necessary to rely on your own judgment and overrule the opinions of others, but don't hesitate to solicit their criticism. They often bring up excellent points worth investigating.

Be sure to keep your sales force advised of the status of your inventory. Insist they keep you informed when stock is low. Make certain they all know when certain merchandise is not available, especially when there is a big demand for it.

In my early years, my clerks would be taking orders for merchandise we no longer had in stock and would promise delivery in a week or two, convinced I could get it by then. On occasion, the manufacturer was no longer making the item, but I had neglected to pass the word along.

Then we'd compound the mistake by not advising the customer who was waiting.

Should this happen to you, by all means phone the customer at

once and explain the mistake, pointing out that it was an honest one and suggest some other merchandise. Admit your error and it generally works out for the best.

Now here's another suggestion that may sound too simple to even consider, but, believe me, this requires constant vigil. I refer to newspaper, radio or TV advertising, but mostly newspapers.

Check everything yourself

Be sure you have checked the prices, the descriptions, the cuts—everything. I know this is the responsibility of someone else, but an error in price can be costly, more costly than you think.

Assign someone you trust, someone close to you, to double check all advertising.

Another point—don't always believe the representatives who call on you or the manufacturers who sell to you when it comes to specifying a delivery date. Don't promote any merchandise until you see those packages come into your building.

I mapped two or three major advertising campaigns and launched them with a flourish only to be advised of a delay in delivery. Sometimes the delay was for a good reason, but, nevertheless, the merchandise was not there when the customers arrived.

This is a terrible blunder and I know buyers will insist it can never happen to them, but you'd be surprised. Sometimes you're tempted to jump the gun. If this temptation hits you, forget it. Don't do it. Wait until the merchandise arrives before selling it, it's as simple as that.

Chapter 13. My little black book

I always kept my little black book right on my desk where visitors could easily spot the title, clearly printed on the front cover: "Preferred Resources."

I enjoyed eyeing my visitors as they glanced at the cover, stretching to read the title. They were curious to know why the book was on my desk and just what information it contained. This was especially true if they were in my office for the first time.

When they discovered that this little black book included the names, addresses and telephone numbers of my "preferred resources" they immediately began asking questions about this list, making every effort to have their names added.

Pick top resources

Probably the most important responsibility of a buyer is to select good resources; they can spell out success and profit. A buyer must be able to separate the good from the bad apples.

So much depends on the type of representative who calls on the buyer. You must be able to read right through this salesman. You must ask yourself: "Does he speak for his company? Is he like his company or is he different?"

Sometimes it turns out that the company is better than the representative and you know you should buy despite the actions of the salesman—actions you may not approve, but which you may be able to correct in some way after you have done business with the firm.

Sometimes you may determine that the representative is a fine, upstanding fellow, but his company does not back him up; therefore, you will have to pass up his line.

Naturally, experience is the best teacher and I always prided

myself on being able to pick them right. When they were right, their names would go into my little black book.

I expected a lot from my resources, but I gave them plenty in return.

I preferred the type of salesman who brought in samples and knew what he was talking about—one who was ready to close a good deal. A good representative is confident of his line and offers it to a buyer because he knows it has quality plus value. A capable salesman should be interested in his account's volume, in a buyer's desire for something unusual, maybe even an exclusive. He must be willing to cooperate in promotions. He must have the enthusiasm to help the buyer put over the product.

For this representative I was always ready to do quite a bit. I would provide him with ample floor space for special displays and I would arrange for a strong advertising program. In addition, I would set up meetings with our sales staff so that the representative might explain his product in full, even permitting him to suggest a sales plan.

Review the line

Every six months I would review the performance of a line. I would ask the representative if we were doing a good job for his company. I would then tell him what my staff and I thought of the item. We could, as a result, work out a more satisfactory arrangement, if one was needed. Cooperation is vital. Good buys are found only on a two-way street: the representative does his part and the buyer does his.

The kind of salesman that irritated me most was the breezy Bill, especially the one who stormed into my office without an appointment. Usually these fellows also tried to high pressure me by overtalking their product. Most often, they were the kind who would promise a delivery date their resource could not meet. This is inexcusable and when this happens a buyer must quickly cut off this contact. If the item is especially good, the factory must be told why no more orders are forthcoming—due to the salesman.

Just as weak in my book are the timid types or the fumblers. Timid Tommy waits for you to ask all the questions and then hesitates in answering them, forgetting many salient points. Fumbling Freddy is the kind who drops his sample, can't find his catalog or the right page in the catalog, even stammers and stutters as he makes his presentation. He takes up too much valuable time and you get nervous just watching his performance.

Even worse, though, is the fellow who tends to become abusive when you refuse to buy or the chap who starts off by trying to impress you with the fact that he is a close friend of a close friend of your boss.

Whenever you are in doubt about a representative or his promises don't hesitate to suggest that a phone call be made to the main office of the factory. Pick up the phone and hand it to the salesman

to check an important price or special deal. You'll soon find out

where you stand and where the salesman stands in the confidence of his firm.

When you are satisfied with the representative and his company, add his name to your little black book and depend on this resource for future business.

Chapter 14. Getting your salesclerks to sell

Many good salesmen figure buying is the responsibility of the buyer only. It's up to the buyer to select the right type of merchandise at the right price and at the right time.

They're wrong.

It's just as important for the salesman to be concerned over the selection of merchandise as it is for the buyer to show an interest in how the goods eventually are sold. They should work hand in hand.

Many buyers feel they need not worry about the sales staff. All they should do, these buyers believe, is to obtain the right merchandise and the selling will take care of itself.

They're just as wrong as the salesmen previously mentioned.

Will it tell?

Buying is really selling—you might call it pre-selling. When you look over samples and consider their value, you actually are thinking of them in terms of sales.

"'Will this sell?" is the question you really ask.

And as you pop that question to yourself, you subconsciously picture how you would sell it. You become excited over some special features, the price, or the promotional possibilities. You envision some advertising that will bring hundreds flocking to your department.

This may take only a second or two. but what you are doing is selling merchandise before you have bought it. When you finally place an order, you see it as already sold.

"How can it miss?" is what you are saying in effect, or why would you be placing an order.

You certainly never buy a product without giving any thought to its sale. You surely don't say to yourself: "Okay, I'll buy this stuff.

Whether it will sell, that's not my business. That's up to the salesmen."

Buying is pre-selling and since you have sold yourself on the salability of an item, you are the best person to pass along that confidence to the sales staff. Therefore, you should be vitally concerned with the salesclerks and their abilities.

Hire your own people

I insisted on hiring my own salespeople. Ours was a big store and we had a personnel department. Applicants would go there first, answer necessary questions and then be assigned to the departments. However, when I protested I was given the opportunity to look over applicants before they were permanently placed in my department. You, too, should be just as interested.

I looked first for personality in my salespeople. Their approach to the customer is most important. Does their personality invite a customer to buy or does it chase him away?

Next I studied the appearance of applicants. Did they dress well? Were they neat? The salesman with run down, unshined shoes, baggy pants and badly in need of a hair cut generally gives the customer the impression that he is careless about everything he does— even his judgment on merchandise. They shy away from salesmen like that.

I always tried to explain the work of our department to new-people. I'd point out there was more to selling than waiting on customers. Knowledge of stock, arrangement of merchandise and an appreciation of the status of our inventory were keys to better sales. When the salesman has a few moments, he should check into all of these and he should keep a live card file of prospects. Phone them on specials.

If an applicant showed the right spark, I'd send him back to personnel and ask that he be assigned to my department. The applicant would then be sent to our store school for a few days to learn the routine and policy, and then he'd come back to me and we'd understand each other. In some of my departments I would send the applicant, after he was assigned to me, to our distributors to learn the product firsthand.

Keep checking on progress

I'd watch the progress of my clerks. We'd hold meetings; we'd consult as often as possible. The buyer should be in close touch with

the sales force. As I've said before, a good sales staff means a smart buyer.

I always looked for extra initiative—the hungry salesperson. I admired the fellow who would step up to me and tell me he had a family and was eager to move ahead. I'd give them chances to come in early, to help me on the telephone, to check stock, etc.

They moved up fast once they got the chance.

I remember a stock boy who came to my attention one day. We were stuck with some used merchandise and trade-ins. He came to me and suggested an auction for store employees only. I pounced on the idea, became my own auctioneer, had a lot of fun and we cleared out all the merchandise.

You never know where the brains come from—stock boy, salesclerk or your own secretary. Always be ready to pick these brains. They'll make any buyer look good.

Chapter 15. What about the customer

There was a time in retailing when buying was sort of a game, where the customer and merchant matched wits and only the customer who was well informed received good bargains. That, of course, has been reversed.

Today keen competition and an informed buying public has been responsible for the change of the merchant's slogan of "let the buyer beware" to "the customer is always right." The store that caters to the customer in quality merchandise and efficient service is the one that can look at a profit at the end of the year.

Informed public

Since the buying public has become informed, it demands more from the store—the latest merchandise and styling, improved services and better informed salespeople.

Our sales staff was briefed constantly on "the customer" and I made every effort to have them well trained and well informed.

Over the many years we have had all types of customers, but the one thing that always stood out in my mind was the fact that a sale could be lost because a customer wasn't handled properly.

I can look back and recall many sales we lost because the salesman used the wrong approach, or he failed to impress the customer with his knowledge of the product. That is where proper training and supervision pays off.

Meet the customer

I have found also that it is a good idea to make yourself available to the customer. Don't hesitate to step in during a salesman's pitch to assure the customer that the salesman's advice is good. Give them the benefit of your seasoned understanding of the product. Nearly always the salesman will say, "that was our buyer," and the cus-

tomer will be impressed with your attention. Or perhaps he is dissatisfied with the treatment he has been getting. Be quick to step in and carefully solve the problem being sure not to blame the salesperson in front of the customer.

It is well to know the types of customers and train your salespeople to sell to them. I would like to talk about just a few I have encountered in my many years of selling.

"Just looking" customer

This customer has a standard catch phrase "No, thank you, I'm just looking."

Is the salesman satisfied to let the customer wander around the department without any attention? Many times he is. Perhaps he gives them his card and says, "When you find something I'll be here."

This is definitely the wrong attitude. A well-trained salesman will be very polite but will suggest that there are some exceptional values he would like to point out that the customer might not notice. Perhaps something is on sale or will be the next day. In this instance, calling the customer's attention to it will arouse his interest. In this way you get him to talk and once the ice is broken you can soon find out in what particular item or model he is interested. If the customer is very insistent on wanting to look around, the salesman should be alert so that when the customer stops to look at a certain item he can be there to explain its value. While the customer wants to be free to look around, I have always felt that if the salesman is there at the right time he will probably make the sale.

Undecided customer

This customer usually says, "Well, I just can't make up my mind."

They are sincere in their inability to make a decision. The salesman has given the customer a lot of time, has shown all the styles or models in which the customer is interested, explained the values and comparisons and still there is indecision. If the salesman is wise he will call his buyer or supervisor to meet the customer for he may have another angle to present, or he may be able to assure the customer about his choice, or may qualify it with the fact that if the customer is not entirely satisfied he may return it. Usually after the merchandise is in the home the customer is completely satisfied.

The silent customer

You have all had this type of customer—usually he just nods his head, but doesn't talk.

He seems to be interested, but not in the salesman. How can you reach him? How are you going to engage him in conversation? This silent customer is either a shopper who only wants to go around and get prices or he is timid and afraid to ask questions. You will soon determine which one, for the shopper usually has a pad and pencil in his hand.

If the salesman is alert he will interest the timid customer in a special value for the day, he will tell him to look around and that he would like to walk with him and point out the values on the floor. This usually prompts the customer to start a conversation and nine times out of ten you will close the sale.

The technical customer

This is the customer who requires skillful handling.

He has made it his business to know about the product and is well informed. It is the job of the salesman to impress him with his knowledge and to satisfy the customer with every small detail.

That is why all salespeople must be well trained and informed. They must realize that every customer can be well informed and that they must be prepared to meet that challenge.

You will have no trouble in making a sale because as soon as he is aware that you know your product and are sold on it yourself the customer will have confidence in you and will be ready to buy.

The comparative customer

This customer usually informs you right at the start that he wants the "best buy."

This is your clue that he has been shopping around and is going to purchase what he considers the "best buy." He has gone to every store, has compared prices, quality and styling and he can quote details. This is probably the greatest challenge to the salesman because here he has to find exactly what the customer considers most important and then sell that point to him.

The fact that the price is lower has to be met by the salesman, too. He must get the customer to tell him where he can make the purchase at a lower price. Then inform him that you will have the item shopped and if the price is lower you will meet it. That price, of course, becomes the price for the item, regardless of the customer.

The shabby customer

When a salesman analyzes the customer and ignores him because of appearance he has made a big mistake. It is true that the way a person dresses may be an indication to his character, but not always.

I remember one incident. I returned from lunch to find a customer in our deluxe showroom looking at one of our highest priced units. He was dressed in overalls, well worn shirt, no hat. He gave me the impression that he might have been a farmer who had come in with a load of produce.

I inquired of the salespeople why he was not waited on and the impression I received was that they didn't think he would buy.

So I approached him and found him responding immediately. I explained the details of the various television models and within a few minutes he had purchased one of the higher priced sets and paid cash for it.

Needless to say that sale was put on the stock book and no commission was paid on it, and it made a good talking point at my next meeting. So don't judge the purchasing power of a customer by what he wears.

I cannot stress too much the importance of the buyer or supervisor to watch his sales force in their methods of selling and continually have meetings where these points are discussed so that the salesman is always aware of the customer.

I always managed to be on the selling floor at the three critical times of the day. At opening time in the morning when the salespeople are prone to gather in groups and discuss their personal affairs and happenings of the evening before; during the lunch hour when the hurried customers come in, and at closing time. This is the time when salespeople are usually so busy making up their books that they fail to see a customer or they don't want to become involved with one for fear they will not have time to close their books and get out when the bugle blows.

Chapter 16. When you think you've arrived, you've ceased to climb

You've all met the buyer or merchandiser who is convinced that he and he alone knows all the answers. I've confronted a number of them in my half-century of buying and selling. Some of them eventually became aware of this failing and corrected it. As a result they rose to greater heights. Others just rolled along until they stumbled and, when they did. there was nobody interested enough to help them up and they were finally eased out of their responsibilities.

Some of these buyers who were having difficulty wearing the same size hat were old timers; some were young fellows trying to reach the top. They placed themselves on a pedestal long before they deserved such elevation. When on that lofty perch, they usually are easily annoyed when anyone dares to disagree, are seldom available for conferences with their employees and, in general, permit an air of hostility to surround their activities.

Cooperate with the sales staff

This is contrary to the objectives a good buyer should try to achieve: mainly, to obtain at all times the full cooperation of his employees, especially the sales staff. He needs the confidence of his staff and this he can obtain only if he allows himself to be human.

He not only should be available to them for advice and exchange of ideas but also should be their counsel on personal as well as business problems. Often an employee may be laboring under a serious personal problem. If the buyer can be consulted, he might be able to help out. If he does, he has found himself a loyal, enthusiastic supporter.

So I urge all buyers to talk to their people, get out on the sales

floor and visit with them, if necessary. Apply adult psychology, which is the same as saying "use common sense."

Personality is important to a buyer. I know some will deny this and say: "Just give me the man who knows his merchandise, can close a big deal, be quick with figures and you can have the guy with personality."

However, I maintain personality helps in winning over the sales staff and, if you can accomplish this, you've got yourself a crew of people who will move the merchandise you acquire and make you look like a smart buyer.

It doesn't cost anything to say "good morning" and "good night." Say it with meaning. It doesn't cost any more to smile than to frown.

Employees quickly size up their boss and if they like him his work is that much easier. A buyer must generate enthusiasm among his staff, his immediate aides and his salesmen as well. A buyer's loyalty is to his company first, then to the product he buys and next to the staff which must sell it.

He must be sold on all segments of his work and when he exudes that confidence in his company, his product and his salesclerks, he'll be a success. A happy family will produce results.

Speak up for your staff

It's important, for example, for a buyer to be concerned about his employees, especially where their finances are involved. If they deserve more money, make every effort to get more for them. On the other hand, if an employee is to be reprimanded save that for a private conference in your office; don't lash into them on the sales floor.

I'll never forget one of the first merchandise men for whom I worked. I couldn't do anything to please him. He'd criticize me in front of everybody, using language definitely not becoming a merchandise man. I'd find myself changing counters around three or four times a day and he'd have me performing other senseless tasks.

One night I went home and told my wife that I'd just about made up my mind to quit. If this fellow once more tried to make a fool of me, I'd let him have it and walk off.

Sure enough, the next morning he started climbing all over me. I reared up and shouted back at him: "I've had it. I've taken all I intend to. If you're so smart and I'm so stupid, you don't need me. I'm quitting."

As I started to stomp away, he called out for me to come back. When I faced him, he smiled. It was about the first time he did that.

"Well," he beamed, "you've finally shown me a little guts. I was wondering if you'd ever have nerve enough to tell me off. I was about ready to give up on you, but now I think you're just the fellow I need. Let's shake."

We shook hands and became close friends.

Maybe his was good psychology, but I don't agree. I insist there are better ways of winning over employees. A pleasant personality is a more effective way.

Don't think you know it all. When you do, there's no place to go. You've ceased to climb when you think you've arrived.

Chapter 17. If I were a small retailer

I know many readers will be saying, as have a number of my friends in the past, "It's easy for you to write about buying. You always were able to buy at the best prices because of your store's national reputation and because of the huge amount purchased. Anybody can do a good job with all that support behind him."

That's true. A buyer for a big department store, big chain organization, or big mail-order operation has an advantage. It is easier for him to get quantity discounts than it is for the little fellow. Most buyers, such as I, accounted for millions of dollars worth of sales. It was only natural for a manufacturer to cater to our whims, though plenty didn't.

What would I do if I were the buyer, or owner, of a small shop?

Basically, I'm sure I'd look for the same type of merchandise, adhere to the same principles, feature similar promotions and sell at the right price. Specifically, here's what I think I'd do if I opened a small store tomorrow or became the buyer for an organization much smaller than the store I represented for more than thirty-eight years:

1 I'd know my cost of doing business. This is of utmost importance. You can't go on if you must guess at your cost of doing business. I'd make sure I was including the complete cost, not just a part of it. You can't buy an item for $6.00, sell it for $10.00 and think you've made $4.00. You must charge against this your over head, your own hours of effort, the cost of bringing the goods in and having them go out—the cost of every penny of expense, no matter how trivial, all adds up.

Only when you know your cost can you buy right and sell right.

2. **I'd know my market and my own potential.** What area did I feel comprised my market? What share of this market could right fully be mine? Within what radius could I perform my best service?

This is a vital point for it will curb any tendency to overbuy. It will discourage trying to buy in large quantities simply to get a better break in price. When you do, you often find yourself stuck with merchandise you'll be forced to give away.

3. **I'd seek out one or two live-wire jobbers in my area.** Wholesalers that have a good, clean stock of leading items, firms on which I could call in emergencies. Jobbers can be your best friends. They save you the time of seeing salesmen, they act as your banker and financial advisor, they serve as your warehouse. They save you the space and the money needed to carry a big inventory.

Even as a buyer who bought more than all the jobbers in my area sold within a year, I still did business with two jobbers nearby. They even handled fill-ins for items which I bought in good quantity. They performed a valuable function for my business, and still do for my company, immense as it is.

4. **I would specialize in certain lines. I** would become known in my area as the man who knows all about a particular line or lines, even to the extent of repairs.

5. **I'd feature trade-ins and rentals.** We did this with great success at Famous-Barr. The smaller retailer's big hope against the discounter is in services which that type of operation can't perform. Trade-ins on all kinds of equipment mean added sales and, eventually, added profits. The same is true of rentals.

6. **I'd want to become a member of some buying group.** If not a buying group, some buying organization, or I'd sign up as a franchised dealer—maybe even go into some cooperative venture. No question about it, quantity buying brings the best prices. The little fellow hasn't a chance unless he works with other little fellows in his area.

Buying together enables the group to take advantage of special discounts, rebates, advertising allowances, etc. Even competitors can find advantages in belonging to the same group, if the price is right. After all, your toughest competitor isn't the man selling the same lines as you do, it's the other stores which are fighting for your share of the consumer dollar. It's up to you and others in your field to convince the public within your market range that your line of goods is important to their way of living.

7. **I'd have the courage of my convictions.** I would try not to be stampeded by what the big fellows were doing or by what the fellow across the street was doing. Naturally, I'd pay attention, but then I'd analyze my own business and act in my own best interests. If fishing reels were selling for $8.90 and I paid $10.20 for mine, I

certainly wouldn't sell them for $8.89. I wouldn't even sell them for $10.50. Maybe $12.50 or $13.00, but no less. I would know the cost of doing business and to sell for less would mean eventual bankruptcy.

I'd lay off that particular line of reels and sell some others. I'd hunt for something similar and almost as good. I would get around it some way. I certainly wouldn't work for nothing.

Spell out your principles and live by them. If you feel like dropping a resource, go right ahead. Don't keep selling items for a manufacturer in whom you no longer believe.

Chapter 18. He started as a stock boy

If Horatio Alger had chosen retailing as his career, he would have started as a stock boy and worked his way to the top. Stock boys are about as far down the ladder as one can go. Most of them are high-school youngsters and many have been forced to disrupt their education because of difficulties at home.

This may seem unimportant to the buyer at a major store, but I insist that concern over a stock boy is all part of the buyer's job, that is, the good buyer's job.

"Keep your eyes and ears open" are the first suggestions you should pass along to your stock boy as you show an interest in him. It is a wise buyer who takes his stock boy in hand and teaches him the basic duties of his assignment.

A stock boy should be reminded that his work kit consists mainly of honesty, cleanliness and an urge to work. I know these are rare ingredients, but they can be found. Encourage your boy to ask questions and, by all means, tell him the value of promptness.

Help him become quickly acquainted with his stock and urge that he find methods of arranging the merchandise for fast movement. He must also be able to keep records and must have complete confidence in his superiors. Encourage him to come to you when he discovers anything unusual.

As the boy demonstrates alertness and an ability to follow orders, he should be entrusted with more responsibility. Often this gives him the incentive to improve the efficiency of your department. As he progresses, be sure to reward his good work.

I've seen stock boys move onto the sales floor and higher up, thanks to proper encouragement from a buyer. Taking stock of your stock boy is one of the wisest investments a buyer can make.

Chapter 19. What's ahead and how to face it

Merchandising is becoming more and more competitive. It's also much more complex, even though stores now boast the latest electronic equipment for quicker bookkeeping for sales records, buying trends, inventories, etc. Because marketing is more competitive and complex it is most exciting and fascinating. While there is something new every day, common old-fashioned horse sense still has its place in the field; at least, so I'm convinced.

What are some of the challenges merchandisers face today?

1. The addition of styling to the buyer's problem of finding the right quality at the right price.

2. The loss of meaning to the words "list price."

3. Discount-house selling.

4. Salesmen vs. self-service.

5. The chances of stockroom boys against the college graduates.

6. Stricter government curbs on advertising.

Let's look at these one at a time.

The trend to styling

As a buyer of more than fifty years' experience, about all I had to contend with during my half-century was quality and price. Was the merchandise of such quality that my firm could continue to stand back of it? Could I get a better price so as to undersell my competitors and make a better profit for my company?

A store that wishes to remain in business more than a few months or years must rely on quality. Your reputation is built on quality. Customers forget price concessions sooner or later but shoddy merchandise is never forgotten nor forgiven. If you make good on poor merchandise, your company soon will be suffering losses in exchanges and adjustments.

More recently, the American public has become style conscious.

It isn't enough to offer quality at the right price; the item now must have the latest styling as well. Maybe the automobiles started it with their change from black to color combinations, and their annual model change-overs. Maybe it is simply our striving for better and brighter things in life. Whatever it is, the customer today wants styling.

Thus it becomes important for the buyer to seek quality, price and styling. Don't let public fancy stampede your judgment. Quality will be remembered long after price is forgotten.

List prices a listless term

What's happened to the list or retail price? Has it lost its meaning? Has the surge of discount selling made a joke of the retail price?

For years, marketing blithefully adhered to its historic markup or margins—40 per cent off to the retailer; 50 and 10 per cent to the jobber; 10 per cent to the salesman and, more often than not, a straight 50 per cent off to the "department stores."

With this staid, old formula as a guide, the manufacturer makes an item, adds the cost of distribution and promotion and arrives at "suggested" list or retail price. It's as simple as that, or is it?

Keen competition started to reduce prices. Soon each factor in distribution found himself compelled to reduce his margin of profit in order to lower the price—to lower the retail price suggested by the manufacturer. Before long, the list price became merely the starting point for price trimming. Eventually, the list price has become worthless; nobody ever sells at that price except, of course, Fair Traded merchandise in states with Fair Trade laws.

Wise dealers disregard the list or retail price. They study their cost of doing business and then buy at a price that permits a fair profit. The buyer must get his purchase price down low enough to make a profit even at a reduced margin.

List prices have become the football of marketing. To avoid being kicked around, a buyer must direct his efforts toward a private brand, an exclusive, or into lines where net prices prevail.

Don't discount the discounters

Each new era of merchandising introduces fresh ideas of competition, yet most have been tried decades before. Fifty to sixty years ago the mail-order houses made their bow and every one screamed. Experts forecast the end of independent dealers.

As soon as the mail-order houses became an accepted form of

competition, chain stores began to spring up and sharp criticism was directed at them. Once again, the independent was said to be doomed, but he managed to live on.

Then along came the catalog houses, a bit different from the mail-order firms because they led the consumer to believe he was "getting it wholesale" and, in many cases, he was. Still the independents struggled on.

This was followed by the superchains or supermarkets which were able to cut costs and offer products for less, much to the irritation of the mail-order houses, the chains and the independent who continued to eke out a living.

More recently it has been the discount house, both open and closed. This for certain, the prophets of gloom predict, will sink the drowning independent and will make life even more miserable for the department store, the chains, the mail-order houses and the catalogs. How can they all possibly survive?

Well, this has been going on as long as America has encouraged free competition. Solve one problem and another pops up. It's what makes our way of doing business so healthy. You can't afford to coast. All those who stay on the job, roll with the punches and pick up pearls of knowledge from these new developments will grow even stronger.

As rival merchants meet the prices of the discounters, the latter must also adjust. All stores are cutting costs, discovering more economical ways of doing business and meeting their competition head on. As their prices are matched the discounters must also add a few services they hadn't scheduled in order to keep customers coming back. This, of necessity, increases their costs of operation. Result? A leveling off of types of business so you won't be able to tell one type of store from the other.

All of which means that the buyer must never become tightly-bound to any one method of tradition. He must change with the times. He should not cry for protection. He should go out and do better. If one fellow can do it, so can he. These are wonderful days for the buyers because ingenuity is at a greater premium when competition is keen than when everything is serene.

Private brands, quality and cooperative buying are some of the best answers to price competition.

Salesmen vs. self-service and automation

Self-service is nothing new. I tried "cafeteria" selling as far back as 1910 in Chicago. It enabled me to sell certain items faster and

without extra help. But did that kill the salesman? Of course not, they are more important than ever.

Modern forms of merchandising are eliminating the need of some employees, but much of this help has been expendable. The able salesman is still in demand and always will be. As Gen. David M. Shoup, Commandant of the U. S. Marines, once said: "The day will never come when the American can lay down his rifle and defend his country with an exotic panel of push buttons."

Like the rifle, neither will the salesman ever be obsolete. It is up to the buyer to assist in the training of better salesmen so as to increase their productivity. No store can afford the lazy salesman or the slow thinker. Self-service will absorb that line quickly, but it won't take the place of the alert salesman.

Stores which train their salesmen properly find them more than worth their pay. Many products require more than just a haven on the shelf; they need selling and only a salesman can do that— not an "exotic panel of push buttons."

Self-service, on the other hand, has a definite place in the store of today and the market place of tomorrow. With the cost of doing business rising, small items must be disposed of through selfservice. This is also true of products constantly in demand and easily understood by the customer.

Yes, self-service is here to stay, but so is the salesman—the good salesman.

Any hope for the stockroom boy?

Or, maybe, I should ask, "Will the college boys take over?" There is no question but what more stores are eyeing the college graduates for their future executive positions. Some stores hire these boys directly out of school and move them into responsible posts after only a short period of in-store training.

I'm of the old school. My alma mater was Know College, but I spell it "K-n-o-c-k-s"—the College of Hard Knocks. I like to see the hustling stockroom boy move up in the ranks or the lowly, parttime salesman get a chance to work up as a buyer. I'm convinced they'll still get their opportunities, but there will be a greater influx of college men, and that has its merits, too.

Any successful business needs good balance, something old and something new. No business should switch radically from one to the other. No business should go 100 per cent automatic, for example. No business should fire all salesmen and substitute pegboard displays.

And no store should rely only on college graduates. Buyers should come out of the ranks of the salesmen as well as from the campuses of our great universities.

Yes, there still is hope for the stockroom boy.

Watch out for Uncle Sam!

With the Federal government watching the retail operations more carefully and insisting on full compliance with anti-trust laws, the buyer of today and tomorrow may feel himself strapped in his operations. It is illegal to receive any special price considerations, advertising allowances or other incentives not available to a competitor of like stature.

But this isn't the end of the world. After all, the law is the law. It's surprising how much can be accomplished even without some "inside" advantages. In advertising, emphasis on quality, exclusiveness, full lines and store image can do an effective job. Better salesmanship and productivity of employees can offset equal pricing. And private brands always are available to the bigger stores.

These are the days where buyers must be better than ever. The electronic computers can't gauge the public's pulse as well as the buyer who mingles with his employees and talks to his customers.

Human judgment will always be at a premium.

Chapter 20. One hundred steps to sales success

Everyone searches for an easy road to success—for some simple formula or recipe. We, who've been through the revolving door that opens to the business world, know there is no such panacea, no paved highway to the top. But in my time, I've detected some steps that are very necessary to any sales success. They are much easier to list than to climb. So for those of you who want a quick, compact summary, try treading these 100 steps; don't miss too many on your way up the ladder:

For the buyer

1. Always have the courage of your convictions.

2. Quality is remembered long after price is forgotten.

3. Brand name merchandise can be profitable.

4. Be first with the newest in your market.

5. Turnover means extra dollars.

6. Package items offer larger volume.

7. Be awake to sleeper items.

8. Replace special items daily or weekly.

9. Merchandise your display tables daily or weekly. Put fast-moving and wanted merchandise priced right out in front.

10. Watch for firms or inventory close-outs.

11. Specialize in special events.

12. Set up sales events two and three months ahead of time.

13. Rely on your trade journals for latest information.

14. Discount houses are here to stay, learn to live with them.

15. Search for exclusives.

16. Buy often, but conservatively; don't overbuy.

17. Watch your old-season merchandise. Get rid of it quickly.

18. Basic controls are necessary on staple stock.

19. Increase your initial markups wherever possible.

20. Work for savings in cost of operation.

21. Establish pleasant relationships with your resources.

22. Be loyal to your private-brand manufacturers.

23. Build confidence between buyer and seller.

24. Factory representatives or salesmen are your best friends.

25. Deal only with reputable firms.

26. Take advantage of manufacturer's programs for exhibits, demonstrations, displays.

27. Visit your factories periodically.

28. Be sure the resource you represent is financially able to back up its warranty.

29. Take advantage of programs for factory experts to spend time in your store to help educate your salespeople.

30. Display your products to best advantage.

31. Display to sell.

32. Dramatize an outstanding value by focusing on one special spot.

33. Use store-wide displays for special events.

34. Use descriptive signs to tell a story about your product.

35. Be publicity minded.

36. Recognize the value of showmanship.

37. Build a reputation for service.

38. Don't boast to your competitor; let sleeping dogs rest.

39. Don't hesitate to visit your competitor regularly for ideas.

40. Build confidence in your product.

41. Keep feeling the pulse of your public.

42. Sometimes old ideas are still the best.

43. Don't underestimate the power of advertising.

44. Hold weekly product meetings with your staff.

45. Stir up enthusiasm within your salesforce on both old and new items.

46. Demonstrations put action into your sales presentation.

47. If a salesman is worth keeping, he is worth paying well.

48. Cash in on the leisure time of the senior citizens.

49. Delegate responsibilities to your employees.

50. Be willing to share your knowledge with your assistants and selling force.

51. Your salesforce should know what your competitors are offering.

52. Let your salesforce know in advance what you are advertising.

53. Be fair to all, show no favorites.

54. Don't just criticize; praise, too.

55. Win the confidence of your employees.

56. Hold the door open for suggestions or complaints from your employees.

57. Know how to get the most out of your sales force.

58. Don't be over-staffed.

59. Don't be too big to ask your personnel for ideas.

60. Your word should be your bond.

For the salesman

61. Sell yourself.

62. Listen as well as talk.

63. Know your product, how it is made.

64. Always be accurate.

65. Show what your product can do.

66. Make it easy for the customer to buy.

67. Be tactful.

68. Be alert for ways to improve your selling and yourself.

69. Be courteous to the customer who doesn't buy; he may come back.

70. Pinpoint the unusual about your product.

71. Never exaggerate your product.

72. A smile costs nothing, but it brings big rewards.

73. Look and act like a successful man.

74. Sell up.

75. Careful sales presentation brings lasting results.

76. Make your product interesting.

77. Maintain a competitive spirit.

78. Know when to stop talking.

79. Customers are not interested in your own personal problems.

80. Be devoted to your job; give a little more than you are paid for.

81. Take plenty of time with customers.

82. Don't oversell.

83. If you promise something, then deliver.

84. Be on time for appointments.

85. Take care of the early and the late customer.

86. Don't be a smart-aleck; listen and you may learn something.

87. Use the prospect card system; it still pays off.

88. Ask questions.

89. Be appreciative.

90. Organize yourself.

91. Don't be afraid to ask for a promotion if you think you are qualified.

92. Impress the boss with your abilities.

93. Knowledge is important to success.

94. Learn how to take it.

95. Let your customer handle the item you are selling.

96. Personality is important.

97. Make friends.

98. You never stop learning.

99. Be well groomed.

100. Work at your job as though it were your own business.

www.ingramcontent.com/pod-product-compliance
Lightning Source LLC
Chambersburg PA
CBHW071800170526
45167CB00003B/1108